ONE THING IS NEEDFUL

FRANCHESCA TIPPIT

Higgins Publishing

One Thing is Needful
Copyright © 2017 Franchesca Tippit. All Rights Reserved.

No part of this publication may be reproduced, stored in a retrieval system or transmitted in any way by any means, electronic, mechanical, photocopy, recording or otherwise without the prior permission of the publisher except as provided by USA Copyright law. The opinions expressed by the author are not necessarily those of Higgins Publishing.

"Scripture quotations taken from the Amplified® Bible (AMPC), Copyright © 1954, 1958, 1962, 1964, 1965, 1987 by The Lockman Foundation Used by permission. www.Lockman.org"

Published by Higgins Publishing
1.877.788.5613 | www.higginspublishing.com

Higgins Publishing is committed to excellence in the publishing industry. The company reflects the philosophy established by the founder, based on Psalm 68:11,
"The Lord gave the word, and great was the company of those who published it."

Book design Copyright © 2016-2017 by Higgins Publishing. All Rights Reserved.
Cover design by Higgins Publishing

The Higgins Publishing Speakers Bureau provides a wide range of authors for speaking events. To schedule an author for an event, go to www.higginspublishing.com.

Library of Congress Cataloging-in-Publication Data
Tippit, Franchesca
One Thing is Needful – Franchesca Tippit – First Higgins Publishing softcover edition – December 2017
   pages cm. 114
Includes index.
ISBN: 978-1-941580-30-1 (sc)   Control Number: 2017961437

1.   Religion: Christian Life – General
2.   Religion: Christian Ministry – General
3.   Religion: Christian Life - Prayer

For information about special discounts for bulk purchases, subsidiary, foreign and translations rights & permissions, please contact Higgins Publishing at 1.877.788.5613 or business@higginspublishing.com * Published in the United States of America.

TABLE OF CONTENTS

Introduction iii

Chapter One 5

   Black and White TV and a Radio ....

Chapter Two 17

   Before You Know It ....

Chapter Three 33

   The Clock Started ....

Chapter Four 41

   Fluorescent Blue Hues ....

Chapter Five 47

   Truth Be Told ....

Chapter Six 53

   Beyond Human Forgiveness ....

Chapter Seven 63

   When the Trump Sounds ....

Chapter Eight 71

A Disneyland Experience ....

Chapter Nine 83

The Roadmap of Life ....

Chapter Ten 91

Knowing His Voice ....

Acknowledgments 103

Index 105

Prayer Line 111

INTRODUCTION

As you begin to read this book it will encourage you. No matter what you have or do not have, what you look like or even how you were raised, God has His mighty powerful hands on you. Even when you feel alone, He is there all the time. For those who do not know Jesus, I want to encourage you to receive Him into your heart. For those who are saved and have a relationship with Christ; keep on reading the Word of God, meditate on the Scriptures to strengthen your faith and starve all your doubts as you continue to seek His face. *One Thing is Needful,* and that is the Word of God. Read it every day so that it becomes a part of your heart.

Chapter One

Black and White TV and a Radio

I sat down to remember my life and how I grew up knowing who God is and going to church every Sunday. I would sing in the choir and my mother was on the usher board. And if she saw us talking or chewing gum, she did not have to move, she cleared her throat, and we knew that we were in trouble. My sister and I were in the choir, and we would swallow the gum and shut our mouths because we knew that momma did not play. Growing up, I was the youngest of six children, four boys, and two girls. I finished and graduated high school and did some college classes. I finished high school and went straight to Texas Instruments and then to Collins Radio Electronics. God is so good. He blessed me to work for Penrod Drilling Oil Company. I had so many good jobs that the Lord allowed me to get. Before I knew it, I was mixed up with the wrong crowd. I needed to tell somebody about my new associates because it was just a matter of time before I would be messed up. Unfortunately, I had to find out for myself the hard way.

I found myself partying a lot, I found myself trying to smoke cigarettes and then trying to get high. And, in no time at all, I was a complete mess, running around at night going to the clubs and going to friends' houses to get high or to just party. At that time, we thought we were really having a good time, and I can remember how much my mother would be upset with me. I also remember how my brothers and my sister were so disappointed in me.

"How in the world has this happened to Fran? We have loving parents who taught us to love God."

I was the youngest child in the family, so I had to grow up realizing that everybody's eyes were on me. Going through my life and turning into a grown woman, I can see a whole lot clearer than when I was younger. I kept my mother praying because of the spirit of darkness that had captivated my life. At that time, my mom was the only one that knew the power of God. She would talk to me all the time, and she kept on praying. I had a mother that never stopped praying for me. My brothers and my sister would be upset with me, but they did not realize that the devil is real, and I needed the mighty hand of God to rush in and deliver me.

And even right now, when we see people taking drugs and alcohol, we talk about them or get mad at them for what they are doing or how they are acting. But you see, they need the mercy of God to fall upon them and deliver them. They cannot help themselves or leave the drugs or alcohol alone, you have to keep praying, and God will deliver them. However, sometimes, people do not realize that it is a Spirit in operation - an evil Spirit, and it is not that person acting up just to be evil.

The book of Ephesians 6:10 says, *"We wrestle not against flesh and blood, but against principalities and powers against rulers of the darkness and Spiritual weakness in high places."*

It is kind of rough when you are bound up by the devil, but God has a way to bring you out and to make you free. God will transform that situation and turn it completely around for His glory. I can remember asking God to keep me safe when I would come home late at night. Here I am, bound by the enemy and still doing wrong in my sins, but I yet knew that the Lord was with me at that time. All that my mother had told me about Jesus, I did not forget that He will not leave me nor will He forsake me. The Word of God says He will be with me until the end of the Earth and if He will be there for me, who can come against me?

I had just left a party and was trying to get from there to the club *wow*... The Lord is truly amazing. He kept me safe and protected me. I realized that days and months passed me by and I was still walking in darkness. Then, one year went by, and it really got bad. Two years later, and time kept right on passing by. But through the midst of me living in darkness and out in the world, God allowed me to see some things while I was in that state of mind.

Is it only the people that run to clubs, that party all the time and those who get high who are bound up and sinning before the Lord? When we have not asked Jesus Christ to come into our hearts and lives, there is no connection to Him. There is no relationship with the Father. So, the very people that are pointing at you and talking against you, whether they are family, friends or neighbors, they all are doing something wrong themselves.

There is no little sin or big sin. A sin is a sin, and it is altogether wrong and against God. We need to take heed of the Word of God that we all have sinned and fallen short of His glory. The Lord, God Almighty, had to set us all free from something. On this particular day, I found myself all alone and very uneasy. I know that my life could be better than this. I was sitting alone in my apartment one day with no one to talk to and nothing but a black and white TV and a radio. So, I began to turn the radio on to hear some music and, suddenly, I listened to this radio station, and a preacher was talking and encouraging the people of God. By the time I turned the radio knob to hear what the pastor was saying, He caught my attention.

"Someone is listening to me right now that needs a friend, will you call this radio station number right now? I am going to read this phone number out three times, and you will never forget this number."

I felt so strongly in my heart that He knew it was me that needed a friend. I felt like everyone was against me and I needed a change to take place in my life. I needed Jesus to show me His hand in my life. So, I wrote the number down after saying it three times and just like the preacher said, I would never forget it! I got a quarter and ran out to the pay phone - in 1993; the pay phones were only 25 cents. I called the radio station, and the man of God answered and said, "How are you today? the Lord told me that you would call."

The preacher spoke to me just like He knew me, "He says that you need a friend," and I said, "Yes, I do need a friend." He began to pray for me and then He invited me to a revival that He was having, and I said "Yes!" He then replied, "Okay, we will pick you up tonight at 6:30 pm." So, at 6 o'clock, He was at my doorbell to pick me up.

I met one of the sweetest women in the world and her brother, Rorey when I got into the van to go to the revival that night. Today, Donna is one of my best friends. We have been in the same ministry all these years. Whatever we have gone through, Donna and I always remained together in the ministry. The Lord has blessed her and me to connect in the spirit as women of God, and she is such a beautiful person inside and out. That night at the revival, the man of God preached, and then he called me up for prayer. When he laid his hands on me and started to pray, the power of God came down upon me like a mighty rushing wind. I have not been the same since that night. I used to smoke cigarettes for about 11 years. I still had cigarettes in my purse on the evening I went to the revival. However, when I left the Church that night, I knew that a change had been made in my life. I did not feel as empty and lonely as I did before even though nothing had changed that I could visibly see.

By the time I made it home, I had realized that I was delivered and set free from cigarettes. I did not want the cigarettes anymore! God had shown up and showed out on my behalf. I told my mother the next day that I no longer desired cigarettes and she said, "God delivered you from them, He has answered your prayers." I am so thankful to God with all of my heart for taking control of my life and changing me for His glory.

The Lord had control of my hands that day, turning that radio dial and the radio station that I heard the man of God on was 1040AM KGGR. The man of God that prayed laid hands on my forehead was used by God. He is Apostle James E. Turknett. He appeared on the radio every day at 2:00 to 2:30 PM. *The Born-Again Hour* under the presiding Arch Bishop Chambers of the 5c Church family. After being touched by the hand of God, I joined the love 5c Church with Pastor James E. Turknett and the Presiding Arch Bishop B. W. Chambers. About 2 years later, the Lord blessed me to be President over the *Born-Again Hour* at 2:00 to 2:30 pm, Monday, Thursday, and Friday. God used me to help others just as I had been ministered to. I was now Minister Fran coming on the *Born-Again Hour* and praying for the people of God that needed a friend, wanted to be saved or just desired someone to talk to. God blessed me to pray and to encourage the people that were calling in on that radio station every day.

Praise be to God, I have my own prayer line to this very day, where we pray Monday-Friday at 9:00 to 10:30 am. I am praying and blessing the name of the Lord with my whole heart. I have been on my prayer line for 18 years, faithfully.

God has taken me from the darkness of this world and showed me His marvelous light. He is such an amazing God! He delivered me from the world to the radio station for the purpose of ministry. The same radio station that the hand of God held my hands to turn to that day when I heard the preacher. God blessed me to come on that same radio station at the same time and give to the people just like what I received that day when I needed a friend. I have found the friend that I was looking for and His name is Jesus. He is the best thing that has ever happened to me. What a friend I have in Jesus.

The Arch Bishop Chambers moved by the Spirit and licensed me as a Minister in 1996. All the glory belongs to God, even when we are not worthy unto God, He still calls us unto His will. I am so thankful to Jesus for the calling on my life. The Arch Bishop Chambers is over the 5c Churches, Christ Charismatic Christian Community Church in Lewisville, Texas and the 5c Revival Center Lake June and Prairie Creek. The Arch Bishop Chambers ordained me at the 5c revival center at the Women's Revival Center. God is so good to have directed my steps for His purpose. I had nothing to do with what the Lord has done for me. I give Him all the glory. The Arch Bishop would work so hard as being our Bishop. We would be at 5c Church on Tuesday night, and He would teach Bible study. On Wednesday night was the ministers' meeting where He taught us how to live in a covenant relationship with God. Teaching us how to preach, and teaching us how to study to show ourselves approved unto God.

I lived in Dallas, but I was in Lewisville every Tuesday night, on Wednesday evening minister classes and Sunday morning worship! I had a strong desire to be used by God for His glory. I was thirsty for Jesus, and my soul was satisfied, in His presence.

The same anointing that was upon Bishop Chambers was upon all the ministers as well; experiencing the awesomeness of God in such a way was so powerful. Even Bishop's daughters, sons, and wife are all highly anointed, and I thank God for them. I am not with the Bishop at this time. However, it is important to give honor where honor is due. And that man of God, Arch Bishop Chambers was a real blessing to me to help me grow.

Chapter Two

Before You Know It

At this time in my life, I am at The Potter's House of Dallas with Bishop, T. D. Jakes. I have been at the Potter's House ever since 1998. the Lord has shown me things amazing things at the Potter's House, to say the least. I see people that God is changing every day in a positive way and they will never be the same. Bishop Jakes is anointed by God and is sold out for the Master's use. He not only preaches and teaches, but he also produces his own movies, writes books, helps people in prison and provides resources for people all over the world through the MegaCare Outreach Ministry of the Church. The Lord has blessed me at the Potter's House to be licensed as a Minister as well. The ministry that goes forth throughout the walls of The Potter's House is life-changing. The presence of God's Spirit that comes into the sanctuary is an experience to be treasured. God gave me the right place and people to worship, with. He put me in the perfect place to learn about Him and to come to know who I am in Him. After God touches your life, you are a brand-new person. God does not let us remain the same He always changes us and our situation. God is the only one that does not change. *He is the same God yesterday, today and forever more.* I am so glad that my God has changed my life and I will keep on running to see what the end will be. You might be saying, *well,* what am I trying to say here?

Well, dear reader, this is the testimony of my life and how the Lord has kept and protected me, and changed and transitioned my life. I know for a surety that when He touched me, He transformed me! There are no more party's and no more getting high. I simply enjoy experiencing the presence of the Holy Spirit.

Nine years ago the Lord dropped in my spirit to write this book in 2008. It is a day that I will always remember, Father's Day. A day that would be forever etched in my heart as I penned my testimony on paper with ink. However, little did I know that my responsibilities would soon change to that of a caretaker. Through taking care of my mother and a myriad of duties, I lost all that I had written down. In efforts to finish this book, I began writing again on May 30, 2014. When I initially started to pen this book, it was on a special day, reminding me of my earthly father whom I'd lost on Father's Day in 1971. Since that time, so many things had taken place in my life.

My oldest brother passed away in 1982. On February 23, 2012, I lost my third oldest brother, who was a disabled veteran. Two months later I lost my mother on May 2, 2012. On October 26, 2013, my youngest brother passed away. God continued to keep my mind and brought me into a new year. I was living the best I knew how for Jesus one day at a time, making sure that I kept reading the Word of God. I have come to a place of realization that *One Thing is Needful*... At all times! We need the Word of God to keep us going, to give us strength and to help us know that Jesus is with us always.

On March 23, 2014, I lost my nephew (the oldest son of my brother who is disabled). My second oldest brother was a Barber who passed away on May 2, 2014. Strangely enough, his life ended the same month and day as my mother. We buried my brother on the 10th day of May. On Mother's Day, my cousin found my mom sister dead on the kitchen floor in her home in Houston, Texas. He called 911, but unfortunately, my aunt had already passed away. The Lord kept our minds even through this!

But then something would happen that would challenge my faith. My eldest son lost control of his car on January 10, 2015. He passed out under the wheel, and he hit a tree flipping his car over three times causing him to be thrown from the vehicle through one of the passenger windows. The doctors said that it looked like my son had a lite heart attack. They kept him in ICU for 5 months and then I had to put Him in a nursing home. God took him home to be with Him in 2017. *He is now In the Arms of a risen Savior.* Thank you, Jesus! My youngest son and I talk about him all the time. I prayed for him, and I continued to go and visit him although it was a 3-hour drive.

Through everything that I have been through, and all that I have seen, I realize that *One Thing is Needful…* I know for a fact that Gods' Word is true because the Word of God has helped me to be strong when I felt weak, it gave me direction when I did not know which way to go.

Some time ago, when I was studying Luke 10:38 references two sisters, Mary and Martha. Martha was more of a servant who cleaned, cooked and showed hospitality to Jesus. But Mary was the woman Jesus had cast out seven demons from her. She knew that Jesus was not like any other man through the power of His ministry of deliverance. Mary wanted to know all about Jesus and to be wherever He was when Jesus opened his mouth to speak a parable, or to talk to the multitudes. Jesus spoke with power and authority, not as a mere man. Martha, on the other hand, was upset and jealous about Mary sitting at the feet of Jesus listening to him speak words of wisdom and teaching as He usually did. Martha was working in the kitchen, and she let it be known that she was irritated.

Luke 10:40-42, *"But Martha was cumbered about much serving, and came to him, and said, Lord, dost thou not care that my sister hath left me to serve alone? bid her therefore that she help me. And Jesus answered and said unto her, Martha, Martha, thou art careful and troubled about many things: But one thing is needful: and Mary hath chosen that good part, which shall not be taken away from her."*

The Lord Jesus gave me a revelation of that scripture; *One Thing is Needful.* You might ask, why is this scripture so important? It is because Jesus is saying if we would meditate on His Word every day, He will lead and direct our steps. Through a relationship with the Lord Jesus Christ, we have access to the Father (God), whenever we spend quality time in His Word and in prayer.

No matter who you are, or what you are going through, know that Jesus is highly recommended! Doctors, Lawyers, Dentists and Fortune 500 Companies are chosen because of their reputation. However, Jesus's reputation supersedes the status of a man, as no one can compare to Him. I recall the times when I look back over my life, and I can see how the hand of God took care of my growing family and me.

Matthew 6:28 says, *"Consider the lilies of the field how they grow they toil not neither do they spin. And yet I say unto you that even Solomon in all his glory was not arrayed like one of them. Wherefore if God so clothe the grass of the field which today is and tomorrow is cast into the oven shall He not much more clothe you, o ye of little faith. Therefore, take no thought saying what shall we eat? Or what shall we drink? Or where shall we be clothed?*

For, after all these things do the gentiles seek for your Heavenly Father knoweth that you have need of all these things. But seek ye first the kingdom of God and his righteousness and all these things shall be added unto you. Take therefore no thought for the morrow for the morrow shall take thought for the things of itself sufficient unto the days is the evil thereof."

The Word of God is saying do not worry about the cares of this world. God cares about you and the things you must deal with each day. If you are going through a difficult situation involving your finances, your health, or possibly a challenging relationship, know that your Heavenly Father already knows about those things that you need. The Lord will work it out and show unto you His mighty hand in every situation. The scriptures remind us that lilies of the field and the birds of the air are being taken care of without them doing anything at all. God will take care of you! Trust the Lord to meet your needs according to His riches and glory by Christ Jesus. Cast all your cares on Him, and He will strengthen you during uncertain times.

Now, when I face a hard situation in my life, I give it to the Lord in prayer. After praying, I keep my mind and heart on Him. Before I began to seek the face of Jesus, I remember thinking that I had to ask someone for help for whatever I needed, whether it be finances or otherwise. If I needed advice about something, I would call friends and tell them about my situation to try and find out what I should do. But as I began to go to Church and hear the Word preached as well as read the Bible for myself, I became more dependent on God alone.

Now, I go to the Lord Jesus Christ knowing that He will help me with every problem that I am facing. He will heal every area of pain and lack, and lead me when I need direction. I have learned to leave my concerns at His feet because He is all-seeing, all-knowing. And because God cares for us, He knows exactly what we need. He has sent so many men and women into my life who preached the Word and prayed with and for me. Those precious vessels of God that I grew up around have strengthened my spirit and have given me a mind to keep on keeping on in Jesus' name. Regardless of my past mistakes and the mess that I had made of my life, the Lord can take a real mess and turn it into something beautiful and brand new. I am a living testimony of what God can and will do for you. I have taken the limits off God because He can do whatever He wants to do when He wants to do it.

Through the pages of this book, I give God the glory because He has opened doors and made so many ways for me to intercede for people on the prayer line. Now, I am praying for people all the time. Everywhere I go, God uses me to pray for others. When I am at home, people call me to pray for them or solely for a word of encouragement when they need someone to listen and speak into their lives. It is indeed a blessing to be used by God to bless others in their time of need. If I had never read Gods' Word, my life would still be a mess. His Word helps us to realize that He is attentive to everything we do or say. Our Savior wants us to pick up our Bibles and read them to get to know Him. That being said, *One Thing is Needful* as He made clear in Luke 10:40-42.

I would not know how to pray or to encourage or just to be a friend to someone without reading the Word of God and applying it to my life. I thank God for calling me to the ministry. Even though I have experienced unbelievable devastation, I understand the weight of the request to pray and to preach the gospel of the Lord Jesus Christ. Yes, *One Thing is Needful*, the uncompromising Word of God. His Word brings peace when you read and meditate on it and gives you strength to stand when facing trying times. As you continue to read the Word, it will become a part of your heart giving you power over situations. However, you must first renew your mind through reading His Word daily. Spending quality time in the Bible will begin to transform your mind to think and act more like Christ. Transformation takes time. However, the positive change in your life is worth the investment. Before you know it, your conversations will be seasoned with salt that brings peace to the hearer, and you will begin to surmount obstacles that were once difficult.

I would never have known how to walk by faith and not by sight without staying in the Word of God. *One Thing is Needful* in our lives because God is soon to come, even quicker than what we might think.

Revelation 16:15 says, *"Behold, I come as a thief. Blessed is he that watcheth, and keepeth his garments, lest he walk naked, and they see his shame."*

Don't you want to be ready when He comes? I know I do! Unfortunately, many people have their minds and hearts on the wrong things. Yes, it's okay to have beautiful things: homes, cars and lovely jewelry, but it's not good for things to have us.

"For what is a man profited, if he shall gain the whole world, and lose his own soul? or what shall a man give in exchange for his soul?" (Matthew 16:26).

We do not need to lose our soul and end up in the *Lake of Fire*. It is vital that we make every effort to do what God has instructed us to do in His Word. But for us to know what He requires, we need to read the Bible that provides instructions of what we should and should not do for our own good. Truth be told, *One Thing is Needful* for every problematic situation we face. *One Thing is Needful* for inner turmoil and devastation. *One Thing is Needful* for eternal life! The Word of God is your map full of directions for everything that you will ever need.

Unfortunately, the enemy does everything he can to keep us busy with mundane responsibilities and distractions that interfere with us meditating on God's

Word. Such as new TV shows and movies that grab our attention, and the latest electronic gadgets, cell phones and the like. Electronics have become a significant distraction for most us, especially the mobile phone that is hard to put down. We take it everywhere. Most of the time it's right at our side within a two-second reach. But the *One Thing that is Needful* (the Bible) is low on a list of priorities until we feel we need it; but that my dear reader is a trick of your adversary. Do not let the deceiver keep you out of your Bible. Decide to read the Word of God daily.

As Children of God it is essential that we take heed to 2 Timothy 2:15, *"Study to show thyself approved unto God, a workman that needeth not to be ashamed, rightly dividing the word of truth."*

The Bible is the literal Word of God that will be our guiding compass for the rest of our lives. We should never take it for granted and recognize its value as God's thoughts too and for His children. He has given us a resource in written form to help us be obedient to His will through the guidance of the Holy Spirit.

It is essential that we take time with the Lord just like we would with our best friend. When we really get to know Him, praise will exude from within us for His goodness and His wonder-working power in our lives from day to day. Nobody can do us like Jesus! Nobody!

Chapter Three

The Clock Started

I want to be ready when Jesus comes. I don't know about you; I want to see His face. I want to hear Him say, "Well done, Fran, my good, and faithful servant. You have been faithful *over* a few things I will make you ruler over many. Enter thou into the joy of thy Lord." We all have a starting date and an end date only known by God before we were born. The clock started to tick the moment we were conceived in the womb. Why do you think that so many people walk through this life failing to plan for their ultimate departure? What do we as Christians have in our hearts to share about the love of God with others that will help them get ready for the end of life on this Earth? The enemy is happy to keep men, women, and children so off focus with distractions that they cannot see the way they are living is leading to their demise. But the reality is death comes to everyone, and the life that you live determines where your soul will dwell for eternity.

If a non-Christian friend or family member asked you what do you believe will happen to you when this life is over; how would you explain eternity and your faith and confidence in God in a way that would make sense to them? If a non-believing family member or friend is drawing close to death and they ask you how to prepare for eternity to meet God; what would you say to them or how would you help and direct them prepare themselves? That is why this book is so essential for me to write because *One Thing is Needful* and it is the Word of God preached that will lead all men who have an open heart to receive salvation through repentance.

Romans 10:8-10 says, *"But what saith it? The word is nigh thee, even in thy mouth, and in thy heart: that is, the word of faith, which we preach; That if thou shalt confess with thy mouth the Lord Jesus, and shalt believe in thine heart that God hath raised him from the dead, thou shalt be saved. For with the heart man believeth unto righteousness; and with the mouth confession is made unto salvation."*

If you have not shared the prayer with an unbeliever lately, why not share it today, and repeat the prayer with them.

Lord Jesus forgive me for all my sins. I believe that you died on the cross and that you were buried. I also believe that God raised you from the dead on the third day. Therefore, right now Lord Jesus, I open the door of my heart, and I receive You into my heart, as my personal Lord and Savior. Thank You, Lord Jesus, for coming into my heart. In Jesus name, I pray. Amen.

Every time that I attend service or watch TBN on TV, a pastor extends the invitation to salvation by asking those in attendance if they would like to accept the Lord Jesus Christ as their Lord and Savior.

I count it a privilege to pray with others for them to receive Jesus into their hearts. It is indeed a blessing to bless others through my walk with Christ, and I am thankful that He continues to meet my needs. I Thank God every day for His grace. Every morning, I thank the Lord for another day that was not promised to me. I thank God for my vision and the ability to walk. I bless the Lord that my heart is still beating and that blood is flowing warm in my veins. He is so worthy to be praised!!!

God wants us to be grateful unto Him for who He is, and not for all the things He gives to us. He wants us to appreciate Him, and not take Him for granted. The Lord always wants us to walk in maturity so we can be an example of Him to show the love and light of Jesus Christ to others.

Philippians 4:4-8 says, *"Rejoice in the Lord always: and again I say, Rejoice. Let your moderation be known unto all men. The Lord is at hand. Be careful for nothing; but in everything by prayer and supplication with thanksgiving let your requests be made known unto God. And the peace of God, which passeth all understanding, shall keep your hearts and minds through Christ Jesus. Finally, brethren, whatsoever things are true, whatsoever things are honest, whatsoever things are just, whatsoever things are pure, whatsoever things are lovely, whatsoever things are of good report; if there be any virtue, and if there be any praise, think on these things."*

Don't allow the enemy to have your mind and become so distracted that you lose your focus. No matter what you are facing, try to keep your thoughts on something lovely, peaceful, and pure. However, times will come where it will be challenging to stay in the right frame of mind. During those times, reflect on the Word of God hidden in your heart so that the enemy will not be able to derail you. It is his desire to make you go backward and not forward. He wants you not to be in right standing with God by influencing you to do evil. However, if you keep your mind on the Lord and His Word, the adversary will not be able to steal your joy. *One Thing is Needful,* and that is quite clear, that we need to stay in God's Word to live an overcoming life.

One area where the enemy attacks us all is in our thought process. Therefore, we must be proactive in preparing our minds for spiritual warfare against the enemy by reading our Bible each day. I know how much the Word is needed because it helps me live according to the purpose and plan of God for my life and to be mindful of the words that I speak.

"But I say unto you, That every idle word that men shall speak, they shall give account thereof in the day of judgment. For by thy words thou shalt be justified, and by thy words thou shalt be condemned." (Matthew 12:36-37).

We will be held accountable to God for our words. It is important to realize how we live our lives and what we say to others matters. We will have to stand alone at the judgment seat and at that time, I want to have more right in my life than all the wrongs. However, doing the right things are based on the roadmap that has already been provided in God's love letter to His Children. If we do not read the Bible, we will not know what we have access to because everything we need to know is written in the Word of God.

"My people are destroyed for lack of knowledge: because thou hast rejected knowledge, I will also reject thee, that thou shalt be no priest to me: seeing thou hast forgotten the law of thy God, I will also forget thy children." (Hosea 4:6).

We can read all kinds of books, but there is no wisdom compared to the Word of God. The Bible has been referred to as *Basic Instructions Before Leaving Earth*. However, to benefit from the treasure of the Word of God, we must open the chest and look inside.

Chapter Four

Fluorescent Blue Hues

I am so glad that the Lord allowed me to turn to that radio station so long ago when I heard the voice of a preacher. I will never forget that the real friend that I needed was Jesus. It was if the clock on the wall stopped just long enough for me to receive Him and began ticking again when I received Him into heart … *tick…tock*! It was time for a change.

I am so thankful and grateful unto the Lord for His mighty miracle-working power. The Lord has provided everything that we could possibly need.

"But my God shall supply all your need according to his riches in glory by Christ Jesus." (Philippians 4:19).

I can understand now why Psalms 103:20 says, *"Bless the Lord ye his angel, that excel in strength, that do his commandments, hearkening unto the voice of his word."*

Even the angels of God move on our behalf when we speak the Word of God over our situations rather than our own words. I recall a time when I would get up some mornings thinking about things that were going on in my life. I would get upset and begin speaking words according to how I felt about the situation. The flesh will have you in a mess! Many times, we speak when we are emotional, especially when we don't agree with something someone has said to us. During periods of trials and testing, we tend to speak words of doubt and unbelief from a place of worry and fear. But, when we come to ourselves through the Holy Spirit quickening us with the Word of God, we are reminded that we shall have whatsoever we say.

I can remember times when I had to encourage myself. I did not have the prayer line or my friends and family around. I had to stand and trust the Almighty God for myself. Sometimes things looked like they would never get better, but God always intervened on my behalf. We cannot continually look for people to encourage, or even to help us to remember that God is our Father!

When we get to the point of our lives when we are going through a storm, we must always remember to try and say the right words. It makes no difference if we are sad, angry or frustrated. We must give our cares to Jesus and concentrate on the goodness of God. I refuse to let my mind stay in a spirit of jealousy and selfishness. I will not allow a lack of forgiveness live in my heart. Because of the strength of an unforgiving nature, it can take over your life and have you regretting the decision not to forgive someone including yourself. So, I have learned to give, ask and to receive forgiveness. It's been a journey, but now I know how to cast my cares upon the Lord because He cares for me. However, that doesn't mean that the enemy won't bring offenses back into your remembrance. But when the offense comes, you will know how to go before God and think about things that are pleasant to Him.

  I recall a time when the enemy tried to distract my mind. I was at home, and I chose to look out of a large window in my living room. I stood right by a beautiful bouquet of flowers as I gazed through the transparent panes at large pecan trees nestled in the lush green grass. The sky was luminous as the clouds bounced against the fluorescent blue hues. At that very moment, my mind rested in the sovereignty of God. Looking for the hand of the Almighty in everything will bring joy in the midst of chaos. That's why I look for Jesus, and I see His handiwork everywhere I go. For example, when I go outside of my house to feed the birds bread or crackers, I am reminded of how God takes care of the lilies in the field (Matthew 6:28). It is comforting to know that He will continue to take care of me because I've sown *seeds of care* because of His love for me.

Sowing is not always money. You can give clothes to help someone that needs them. You can sow your love and time for someone that is heartbroken. Praying for people or a person is a way of sowing.

Whatever you do for, or, to others will come back to you whether it is a right or wrong thing. When we were in sin letting the devil have his way with us, we often reaped what we sowed in the world. But the grace of God provided a way for us to be set free from some of the consequences of detrimental behavior; just like He did with Mary Magdalene. Jesus did not care what man thought about her. God created her, and He was not about to give up on her. Mary became a devoted follower of Jesus and one of the several women who traveled with Him everywhere He and the disciples went. It might not have seemed right for a single woman to be going with a group of men, but she was thankful to God for setting her free. From the time that Mary was delivered from a host of demons, she continued serving Jesus right up until His crucifixion and burial.

I believe He allowed Mary to be the first one to see Him in His resurrected form because of her love for Him. Others gave up on her because of the state that she was in, but Jesus never gives up on anyone! Even when our lives are in a state of chaos, God will be *the stillness in the storm*, and bring peace to our minds.

Chapter Five

Truth Be Told

As we live from day to day, there is a lifestyle that the Lord wants us to reflect, not just doing what our neighbors or our friends are doing. But Jesus says in His Word as we submit to Him that the Holy Spirit will operate in and through us. He will give us the power to change things in our lives for the better. But to live a victorious life, we must first ask Jesus to come into our hearts as our Lord and Savior. We must come with a heart unto God saying, Lord, I repent for all my sins and all my evil and wicked ways. Once we make the transition from living the way that we choose, to living as God says; we can boldly approach the throne of grace in Jesus' name. During your time in prayer talking to God and spending time with Him, lay all your concerns at His feet because He cares for you. Our Heavenly Father is so gracious and kind to us. Going to church and hearing His Word is just another added blessing of being a Child of God. I always ask the Holy Spirit to speak to me when I am getting ready for church. Once service begins, I ask the Lord to speak a word to my heart as I listen to the man of God preach. In this day and time, people are turning away from the things of God, not realizing what is happening. The enemy distracts people so that they cannot see what is really going on.

But the Word of God tells us that we need to be anchored in our faith. We must be steadfast and *unmovable* always abounding in the work of the Lord. Even when it appears that others are having fun living according to their own flesh, choose *life,* not death! For wide is the gate and broad is the way that leads to destruction. I was on my way to destruction until I made a choice to *live!* Oh, how I thank God for moving by His Spirit and changing my entire life through His Word… (wow)!

Praying to God need not be eloquent, it just needs to be from the heart. I remember so vividly when I first cried out to God in prayer, as I still do to this day. I cry out to the Lord asking Him when He moves in the atmosphere to let me be a part of what He is doing in that moment and season of time. I humbly ask the God to add my name to the *Lambs Book of Life*. I say to the Lord, help me, Jesus, to live my life righteously before Your eyes. I want to make it through the doors of heaven. I do not want to spend eternity separated from God in the abyss of the *Lake of Fire*, and I am sure neither do you!

After going through my life of getting high and living that messed up life, I have come to realize the whole truth that God had mercy on me. I am so thankful that I am alive today with a renewed and changed mind. I know that God loves me so much that He gave me a second chance to come to myself. And He will offer you another opportunity as well so that you will be ready when Jesus comes. *Don't wait until it's too late.* It's clear by what is happening in the world that Jesus is coming back soon.

Not only did Jesus take me from the darkness of this world, but He was leading me into the ministry as He filled me with His *mighty Spirit.* Early in my ministry of seeking the face of Jesus and enjoying the change that had a come over me and His peace, there was a shift. There were so many car wrecks that started to take place. The enemy wanted to stop me in whatever way He could, *but God* kept me through them. Those accidents tore up and damaged my cars. But God held His hands on me!

I remember like it was yesterday even though it was quite some time ago (October 28, 1998) an eighteen-wheeler turned out too wide colliding with me and my Dodge Shadow. You would think my life would have ended at that point! Oh, but God kept me amid death. His hand on my life is evident. Truth be told I am *a living testimony*, yes, I am and God is better than good... I give God all the glory because He is worthy. I don't know about you, but I've got to tell somebody about Jesus and what He has done for me. All the things that have taken place in my life and I am *still standing!* One thing I know is that God is no respecter of persons. He's been good to me, and He will *be good to you!*

The Word of God declares that God is the same yesterday, today, and forevermore. He is consistent in His love and grace to help us during difficult times in our lives.

Psalms 50:15 says, *"Call upon Me in the day of trouble; I will deliver you, and you shall glorify Me."*

He is waiting for you!

Chapter Six

Beyond Human Forgiveness

If we ask for something we must first believe to receive it. So, I have requested the Lord to help me to be obedient to His Word to gain eternal life with Him. I have asked the Lord to help me pray, read and study His Word daily even when my flesh wants to do something different. I need Jesus' help to be focused on Him and His plan for my life so that I am not distracted from fulfilling my purpose. Oftentimes, the cares of this world tend to creep up and derail us from God's intentional plan. But He gives us instructions throughout the Bible to pray and to speak the Word to defeat the enemy:

I Thessalonians 5:4 says, *"But ye, brethren, are not in darkness, that that day should overtake you as a thief. Ye are all the children of light, and the children of the day: we are not of the night, nor of darkness. Therefore let us not sleep, as do others; but let us watch and be sober. For they that sleep sleep in the night; and they that be drunken are drunken in the night. But let us, who are of the day, be sober, putting on the breastplate of faith and love; and for an helmet, the hope of salvation."*

I Thessalonians 5:16 says, *"Rejoice evermore. Pray without ceasing. In everything give thanks: for this is the will of God in Christ Jesus concerning you. Quench not the Spirit. Despise not prophesying. Prove all things; hold fast that which is good. Abstain from all appearance of evil."*

Each day that God sees fits to wake me from sleep, I want to start my day in right standing with

Him. When I have a conversation with someone, I want to be a witness of the Lord Jesus Christ.

Being an effective witness requires that we speak in love as we encourage others no matter who they are. After leaving our presence, they should know and be inspired by what we have shared with them. In the evening when it's time to rest, it is my desire to be at peace with myself and the Lord. I know for a surety that ... *One Thing is Needful*, and that is the Word of God; I share it with others rather than using words that do not produce life.

Proverbs 18:21 says, *"Death and life are in the power of the tongue and they that love it shall eat the fruit thereof."*

In whatever way that we speak it will come with power; whether it is life or death. Watch how you talk and think about what you are going to say before you say it. When words are spoken, they are released into the atmosphere and cannot be rescinded. How would your life be different if you could take every bad attitude or hurtful word back? How would you feel if you could have all your past mistakes and mess-ups erased?

As far as erasing what you've said to others, that is not possible once spoken. However, you can ask them for forgiveness and pray that in time they will extend mercy. But if they choose not to, there is *hope and restoration beyond human forgiveness.*

When we fall short and repent (turn away from) our evil deeds and ask God for forgiveness, He will pardon our sins and remember them no more. Jesus makes way for us to live an abundant life. His *grace* provides life, health, and strength to us daily. Regardless of our many mess-ups, our hearts continue to beat as evidence of His saving grace. I want so much for the Lord to be pleased with me no matter where I go or what I am doing. I often ask Jesus to let His light shine through me through the words that I speak, and the life that I live.

We can teach and preach, sing songs and write poems. However, we must also pray and trust the Lord to help us with our family. Keeping our household in order should be our priority. Our children should know that we love them. I am so thankful to God for my two sons whom I love dearly. I'm even more grateful for the love they have expressed to me. You see, life hasn't always been comfortable but through it all, I have come to know that *One Thing is Needful,* and that is the Word of God.

The Lord might not come and move as we want Him to but He is always on time. He knows what to do and what is best for us. God is still in control. Whatever is going on in your life, God is able. He is the *Master Controller,* the *Mighty God,* the *One,* and only *Powerful God!* There is nothing impossible for Him.

Matthew 19:26 says, *"But Jesus looked at them and said to them, with men this is impossible, but with God all things are possible to Him who believes."*

He is the God that can do anything but fail!

Mark 11:24 says, *"Therefore I say unto you, What things soever ye desire, when ye pray, believe that ye receive them, and ye shall have them."*

It is my desire that my entire household is saved, and my confession is that we will all serve the Lord. I thank Jesus for touching and keeping my two sons and turning their lives around. I thank Him for saving my entire family. I believe that the miracle I have asked the Lord for in prayer is already answered. I confess that my whole family is walking in relationship with the Lord Jesus Christ. We must have faith in the promises of God no matter what we see with our natural eyes. *Believing in the unseen is the evidence of our faith.*

God wants to do new and incredible things in your life! Your speech will determine what does and does not happen. Your words have power as to what will manifest, good or bad. If you want the best of what the Lord has for you, the very words that you speak must agree with the promises of God. When your words reflect what God says, that's when He will shift the atmosphere just for you!

Whatever your life looks like right now is how you have been speaking out of your own mouth. Remember death and life are in the power of the tongue. (Proverbs 18:21). The next time you are talking with someone speak kind and loving words and share the Word of God as He leads you. Will it be always easy? No! But with God, *nothing shall be impossible to those who believe!* (Luke 1:37). We are not created to lose or fail. We are purposed to be victorious. We have power over the enemy if we stay in the Word of God and use the Bible as our weapon to fight.

We are so blessed that Gods' presence is all around us. We stand, on a solid foundation of the Word of God. He has favored us in keeping us in every area of our lives by making a way where there appeared to be no way. Know that everything that has been spoken over your life shall come to pass. God is ready to show himself strong in your life no matter what has happened. God gives power to the faint and the broken-hearted. He wants you to be encouraged in Him. Whatever you are dealing with, Jesus is the *Answer!* He is the source of *healing, deliverance, restoration miracles, new beginnings, and second chances.*

We all know about lifelines that the Lord gave to us so many times when we stepped out of His perfect will. God wants to bless us to live the life that His Son died for us to experience. It is His will that we prosper and be in health even as our soul prospers. The only person that can stop you from being blessed is you. God has not brought you this far to leave you.

Hebrews 13:5 says, *"Let your conversation be without covetousness; and be content with such things as ye have: for he hath said, I will never leave thee, nor forsake thee."*

God will be with us unto the end of the Earth and if He is for us who can come against us. He has given us a roadmap to all the blessings with our name on them. No matter what we are facing, we must remember to speak according to His Word and to be *grateful* for what He has already provided.

God rewards those who seek Him, not those that lay around and do nothing. He rewards those that study the His Word to be like Him and to do what He is asking. Our blessings are in the Word of God because the Word is alive. It takes courage to do what God says for us to do. I know how difficult it can be to stop doing things that are contrary to His will, let alone associated with the wrong crowd.

However, when we make a conscious decision to give God our hearts and everything that goes along with it, we cannot lose when we trust Him with our life. I am persuaded that if we are filled with the Holy Spirit, He will give us the power through applying the *Word of God* to live as overcomers.

Chapter Seven

When the Trump Sounds

When God spoke everything into existence; He had a plan in mind from the very beginning. He knew that we would need the *power* to say no to sin. When we are filled with the *Holy Spirit*, we will not be derailed so quickly by the temptations of the flesh. The *Comforter* who is also the *Holy Spirit* will warn us before we do something that we should not do. He will also quicken us to be mindful of what we say. I am so thankful that the *Greater One* who dwells on the inside of me helps me by keeping a guard over my lips! Thanks, be unto God who always directs me in the way that I should go. I am grateful unto my Lord and Savior Jesus Christ for saving me. I do not take His grace for granted. He didn't have to Call, save or deliver me, but He did! When I think of how He pulled me out of the darkness that I was living in, my heart sings Hallelujah! I am no longer a prisoner of sin. I have been *set free* because Jesus brought me into a place where I can see His light!

2 Corinthians 3:17 says, *"Now the Lord is that Spirit: and where the Spirit of the Lord is, there is liberty."*

When you are *set free*, you want the whole world to know that you are no longer bound. You want God to be exalted because nobody could have delivered you but Him. If nobody else praises God, I will bless the Lord always; even if I must do it all by myself! He has been *better than good and awesomely great!*

But even though God loves everyone, many have not received Him into their hearts. Instead, sin abounds much more than what is right and just. It is apparent that Christ is soon to come because the love of many is turning from warmth to ice.

"All these are the beginning of sorrows. Then shall they deliver you up to be afflicted, and shall kill you: and ye shall be hated of all nations for my name's sake. And then shall many be offended, and shall betray one another, and shall hate one another. And many false prophets shall rise, and shall deceive many. And because iniquity shall abound, the love of many shall wax cold. But he that shall endure unto the end, the same shall be saved." (Matthew 24:9-13).

The world is not going to get better as times go by the worse it will become. We need to get in the Word of God to strengthen our faith and strengthen our spirit. As we continue in His Word, we will be able to handle difficulties and know what to do when the trump sounds!

As I read the Bible and it speaks of the day of the Lord; in my mind and in my heart I wholeheartedly want to enter the doors of heaven and spend eternity with God.

2 Peter 3:8-12 says, *"But, beloved, be not ignorant of this one thing, that one day is with the Lord as a thousand years and a thousand years as one day. The Lord is not slack concerning his promise, as some men count slackness; but is longsuffering to us-ward, not willing that any should perish, but that all should come to repentance.*

But the day of the Lord will come as a thief in the night; in the which the heavens shall pass away with a great noise, and the elements shall melt with fervent heat, the earth also and the works that are therein shall be burned up. Seeing then that all these things shall be dissolved, what manner of persons ought ye to be in all holy conversation and godliness, looking for and hasting unto the coming of the day of God, wherein the heavens being on fire shall be dissolved, and the elements shall melt with fervent heat?"

You might say, Minister Fran why are you talking about the end of the world? *Well,* the reason why I bring this up is that at the end of the day, *The Day of the Lord* will come. No one knows the time or the hour. No one knows when their number will be up, or the time of their departure. So, it is essential to be in a relationship with Jesus to be ready when He comes.

The Lord has given many opportunities for us to be saved, sanctified and filled with the precious Holy Spirit. He has provided us with what is necessary for us to be in right relationship with Him. *One Thing is Needful,* and that is the Word of God. The Bible is our roadmap that contains directions for living according to the principles of Jesus Christ.

Titus 2:11-14 says, *"For the grace of God that bringeth salvation hath appeared to all men, Teaching us that, denying ungodliness and worldly lusts, we should live soberly, righteously, and godly, in this present world; Looking for that blessed hope, and the glorious appearing of the great God and our Saviour Jesus Christ; Who gave himself for us, that he might redeem us from all iniquity, and purify unto himself a peculiar people, zealous of good works."*

Jesus gave Himself for us. He loves us so much that He laid His life down that we could be saved from death. Once we receive Him into our hearts and begin reading His Word, our minds will be renewed and our spirits refreshed; as it is with a new Christian. Babes in Christ learn and grow in the love of God throughout their lives. If anyone tells you there will be happy days every day after you become a child of God, they are wrong.

There will be many streams to cross, many trials, tribulations and tests of your faith. Just remember our Father will never leave you or allow you to endure more than you can bear. We as children of God trust Him and have the faith to believe that He will take care of us. Even when it appears that the streams will overtake us, they will not become anything like the rivers we once had to cross on our own. As you become stronger in your walk with the Lord through learning His Word, torrents will become smaller and smaller. As you continue in His Word, your ability to stand during difficult times will be strengthened.

CHAPTER EIGHT

A DISNEYLAND EXPERIENCE

We are born with a purpose set in motion by the Creator of all mankind. The Word of God is the one and only book that can help you tap into your destiny. John 6:63 says, *"It is the spirit that quickeneth; the flesh profiteth nothing: the words that I speak unto you, they are spirit, and they are life."* The Bible gives us a choice in the middle of a world that surrounds us with death. He provides us with the option of choosing an abundant life instead of a life that leads to separation from God. It's easy to be tricked into selecting a life that leads to death through the cunning ways of the devil himself. But, regardless of how *deceitful* he is, we don't have to be his victim. The Word of God is our way out of the worlds death cycle.

Jesus prayed on our behalf to the Father in John 17:17, *"Sanctify them through thy truth: thy word is truth."*

Sanctify means to separate unto. Once you are saved, you are separated spiritually from the kingdom of darkness and born into the kingdom of light. God's Word separates us from the death of the world and places us in the flow of life with Him. Your life will be transformed when you allow the Holy Spirit to come in and give you the power to walk in God's ways. As you let the Word be first place in your life, you will find yourself replacing things that bring death and sin; with things that bring life and peace. There is no limit to what God can do in and through our situations and circumstances no matter where we are. As we continue in the Word of God, we will begin to separate ourselves from sin and choose to be vessels of honor acceptable for God's use. (2 Timothy 2:21).

God's word planted deep in our hearts and spoken from our lips is powerful.

"So shall my word be that goeth forth out of my mouth: it shall not return unto me void, but it shall accomplish that which I please, and it shall prosper in the thing whereto I sent it." (Isaiah 55:11).

Decide to put the Word first place in your life. God will not make the decision for you. He's given us His Word and power through His Spirit, but He does not force us to obey Him. His patience is evident His deep love for us. We all need to be thankful for how much He loves us because there is no love like the love of Jesus. I am so glad that Jesus first loved me when I was yet in my sin and He drew me by His mercy and grace. It didn't matter that I was a mess,

He loved me anyway, and I am still growing and learning the ways of the Lord. Well, dear reader, that's the Christian life in a nutshell, isn't it?

It seems to me that most of us in the family of God ought to admit that we are yet developing in our Christian walk. Going from one state of growth to the next is a process. Therefore, there is nothing to be ashamed of. Just keep in mind that sometimes the process is painful. Even though going through difficult times will come, Jesus will be with you every step of the way. No matter how harsh it may seem, keep the faith, and you will have the victory. Jesus wants us to press on and be accountable for what we do and do not do. Living a Godly life is not a Disneyland experience or a walk in a beautiful rose garden, neither is it living on cloud nine always doing your own thing with whomever you choose.

The Apostle Paul says in 2 Corinthians 4:8-10, *"We are troubled on every side, yet not distressed; we are perplexed, but not in despair; Persecuted, but not forsaken; cast down, but not destroyed; Always bearing about in the body the dying of the Lord Jesus, that the life also of Jesus might be made manifest in our body."*

Persevering through the afflictions, the crushing's, the blast of life without despairing and giving up. I cannot imagine a better picture of the race of life. Winning isn't merely a matter of coming in first. The victory depends on us getting to the finish line with the light inside of us still burning bright. That presence of Christ within us is His gentle and quiet *spirit,* full of peace and hope that stays alive even when darkness is all around us.

Keeping the torch lit often requires running for Jesus and being determined to win! No other option should be our priority or concern. Whatever it takes to keep our spirits high and on fire for God should consume us. God wants us to cross the finish line with our torches still burning bright.

No matter what I've been through the Lord Jesus Christ has made the difference. My family did not realize that I would one day be used by God, just like He will move in your life as well. The Lord has a plan for your life, and He will finish the work that He has begun in you and me. I am not saying that it will be easy, but the Holy Spirit will give you the strength and the resolve to forget those things that are behind so that you can press toward the call on your life by faith. When you are in a different situation, and you don't know what to do, just remember that you are set apart for the Master's use. He will give you revelation into His Word so that you can continue to walk by faith and not by sight, even in difficult times.

Hebrews 11:1-3 says, *"Now faith is the substance of things hoped for the evidence of things not seen. For by the elders obtain a good report through faith we understand that the worlds were framed by the Word of God, so that things which are seen were not made of things which do appear."*

To progress as a Believer, we must have a solid foundation, and there is no foundation apart from faith in Christ. If you are *standing* on the solid rock (Jesus Christ), nothing will be able to come against what you believe; any other foundation is like sinking sand. Do not get distracted with vain imaginations, temporal feelings or artificial joy because vanity exists in the lust of the flesh.

We are told that the Word of God shall live forever, and not one jot or title of the Word shall fail. It helps me to know that I am living and moving by faith according to the knowledge of the principles of the only true God. As we open ourselves to divine revelation and get rid of all things that are not of the Spirit, we will begin to mature in the words of God. Therefore, with the audacity of faith, we should submit ourselves into the hands of the God's divine plan.

Through a relationship with Christ, we enter into a beautiful place of rest by faith and trust in Him. Your confession of belief in Christ is evidence of your faith when you open the door of your heart and receive Him.

Revelation 3:20 says, *"Behold, I stand at the door, and knock: if any man hear my voice, and open the door, I will come in to him and will sup with him, and he with me."*

What will happen if we open the door by faith? There is no limit to what God can do!

"Now to Him who is able to [carry out His purpose and] do superabundantly more than all that we dare ask or think [infinitely beyond our greatest prayers, hopes, or dreams], according to His power that is at work within us; to Him be the glory in the church and in Christ Jesus throughout all generations forever and ever. Amen." (Ephesians 3: 20).

When we began to read the Bible, we will not be moved by everything we hear, but receive only sound doctrine from those who are over us. Also, studying the Scriptures will help us to know when someone is or is not in error. We can only be competent witnesses when we share where the Lord has brought us from and communicate the Gospel with clarity. We must be mindful to live upright as a testimony to the life of faith that we now live. If the way that we live is contrary to our profession of hope as ministers, we crucify Christ afresh causing others to stumble.

Our lifestyle must match what we confess. Though at times it may be difficult to keep the faith because of trials and tribulations, we must endure and persevere. We must hold fast to our profession of faith with all diligence. Do not let the testing of your faith exhaust your energy. Always remember, God will not put more on you than you can handle.

Oftentimes, opposition comes to strengthen your faith. It is during times of crushing that you can choose to access the wisdom of God to be a blessing to someone. Speaking words of encouragement to a friend or family member, or perhaps even a stranger can make all the difference in the world. Stepping outside of the situation to tell someone about Christ will take the focus off what we are going through, and place us in the position of servanthood. We then can effectively minister to others through times of crisis as we continue our walk of faith. Is it easy? Not always. But it is what we as Believers must do daily. We must take up our cross daily by following the voice of Christ and meeting the needs of others. Our faith need not be stagnant but on fire, active and contagious. We need to ask the Lord to create a hunger and thirst in us to win souls for His kingdom. I am learning to let the Holy Spirit lead me to be consistent in telling others about Christ and not to be high-minded.

It takes a spirit of patience when sharing the love of Christ with people. There is a unique way to talk to the lost. We must be careful to speak with love and kindness when witnessing regardless of how cold and callous someone may be. When people are not saved, they can talk to you harshly.

Don't take it personally it's just a result of a sinful world. I am a living testimony of how the enemy uses people to speak hard and cold to each other. We all need Jesus, and that's a fact! The inward witness will grow to maturity only as we continue to stay in God's Word, for *One Thing is Needful!*

Chapter Nine

The Roadmap of Life

The Bible is not just a book, it is a God-breathed, God indwelt, and God inspired. If we read every day, we will begin only to seek what is promised in God's Word. Everything that we need is written throughout the pages of the roadmap of life for us. God has provided lessons and examples for us through the lives of those before us. We can learn from the experiences of Apostles, Teachers and everyday people in Scripture. It is a blessing to know that even though they made mistakes that God kept working with them as He will continue to work with us.

"Being confident of this very thing, that he which hath begun a good work in you will perform it until the day of Jesus Christ: Even as it is meet for me to think this of you all, because I have you in my heart; inasmuch as both in my bonds, and in the defence and confirmation of the gospel, ye all are partakers of my grace." (Philippians 1:6-7).

Through the consistent study of God's Word, we learn:

- How to live by faith
- How to combat the spirit of fear
- How to deal with grief and sorrow

We also learn about:

- The Grace of God
- The healing power of Jesus

- The power of the Spirit of God in us
- The joy and hope we have in Jesus
- The power of *Agape Love*
- How God inhabits the praises of His people
- How prayer connects us with God

Through the Scriptures, we can experience all that God has for us, and through prayer, we can enjoy communication with Him. Prayer is talking to God and listening to what He is saying to us to guide and direct our lives. It is essential that we spend quality time in the Word of God to learn about all that God has for us in this life and the life to come. How can we know about the promises and blessings of God, if we do not read His Word? He has taken the time to give us a roadmap that provides directions to all that He has for us. All we need to do is read the map to find out about the prosperity of God through giving to the kingdom of tithes and offerings. Our financial position is directly related to our giving.

Malachi 3:8-10 says, *"Will a man rob God? Yet ye have robbed me. But ye say, Wherein have we robbed thee? In tithes and offerings. Ye are cursed with a curse: for ye have robbed me, even this whole nation. Bring ye all the tithes into the storehouse, that there may be meat in mine house, and prove me now herewith, saith the Lord of hosts, if I will not open you the windows of heaven, and pour you out a blessing, that there shall not be room enough to receive it."*

The Bible helps us to have right standing with God and to know who we are in Him. We are created in His image with a spirit, soul, and body to reflect His love in earthen vessels.

Mark 12:30-31 says, *"And thou shalt love the Lord thy God with all thy heart, and with all thy soul, and with all thy mind, and with all thy strength: this is the first commandment. And the second is like, namely this, Thou shalt love thy neighbor as thyself. There is none other commandment greater than these."*

God does not leave us to figure things out for ourselves, nor does He allow the enemy to defeat us. We are assured through the Scriptures that Satan is a defeated foe and that we have authority over him!

Luke 10:19, says, *"Behold, I give unto you power to tread on serpents and scorpions, and over all the power of the enemy: and nothing shall by any means hurt you."*

To maintain our position of authority, we must continue to forgive others as Christ has forgiven us. God will not forgive us our trespasses if we do not forgive others. We cannot have our prayers answered while still holding grudges in our heart at the same time. Unforgiveness will clog the channel of blessings and keep you powerless against the challenges in your life. If you have been praying for something and you just can't seem to get an answer, check your heart for unforgiveness! Ask the Holy Spirit to bring to the surface anything that could hinder your relationship with God. Ask Him to reveal any grudges, unforgiveness or self-righteous attitude that you may have about someone or something, and to help you let it go! Once you have genuinely released the spirit of unforgiveness, you will see things you've been praying about come to pass. The word of God shows us how we can take our burdens to the Lord and leave them with Him.

1 Peter 5:6-7 says, *"Therefore humble yourselves under the mighty hand of God [set aside self-righteous pride], so that He may exalt you [to a place of honor in His service] at the appropriate time, 7 casting all your cares [all your anxieties, all your worries, and all your concerns, once and for all] on Him, for He cares about you [with deepest affection, and watches over you very carefully]."*

No matter what you are going through it is not wise to try and make someone be who you want them to be. However, it's nice to show the love of Christ through the joy that He has planted in your heart.

Through your contagious joy, others will be won to the kingdom of God.

Proverbs 17:22 says, *"A merry heart doeth good like a medicine: but a broken spirit drieth the bones."*

Always keep in mind that God is all-seeing and all-knowing, and we are to be examples of His grace, especially if you are called into ministry. God holds those who are chosen to serve in the five-fold ministry to a higher standard of Holy living. If we expect to win the world for Christ, we must depend on the continual infilling of the Holy Spirit. The infilling of the Holy Spirit will cause us to yield to His indwelling presence to impact worldwide change. We must not be satisfied with mediocrity, barely reading our Bibles, and praying every now and then. It will take discipline and commitment on our part, but it is imperative for transformation.

"And if the Spirit of Him who raised Jesus from the dead lives in you, He who raised Christ Jesus from the dead will also give life to your mortal bodies through His Spirit, who lives in you. So then, brothers and sisters, we have an obligation, but not to our flesh [our human nature, our worldliness, our sinful capacity], to live according to the [impulses of the] flesh [our nature without the Holy Spirit]— for if you are living according to the [impulses of the] flesh, you are going to die. But if [you are living] by the [power of the Holy] Spirit you are habitually *putting to death the* sinful *deeds of the body, you will [really] live* forever. *For* all who are *allowing themselves to be led by the Spirit of God are sons of God.* (Romans 8:11-14).

If we, through the Spirit, mortify the deeds of the body, we shall live a life of freedom, joy, and blessings through hope in Christ and service to others. We only need to follow the roadmap of life.

Chapter Ten

Knowing His Voice

Hearing what God says and trusting Him starts with knowing His voice. We come to know the Lord by meditating on His Word and spending time talking to Him in prayer. Though ample time in the scriptures we can then rehearse the promises of God and encourage one another in the Lord as well as our self. Knowing the voice of God is key to our spiritual development.

John 10:27 says, *"The sheep that are My own hear My voice and listen to Me; I know them, and they follow Me."*

When we follow Jesus, we express our belief and trust in Him to be who He says and to do what He says He will do. Our confidence is in the truth of God's Word; it doesn't matter what the circumstances look like, what lies the enemy tells, are even how we feel. Trust is not just an ordinary word; it is an action word. Trusting in the Word of God will change your mindset, how you speak and cause you to experience victory in every area of your life

When you believe God with every area of your life, prepare to experience new challenges and opportunities. Each new day will bring exciting moments. When you rely on Gods strength and not your own power, greater triumphs will come when you trust God to fight your battles, and you will have success every time. You will see new levels of peace and joy. You will begin to experience the abundant life Jesus came to give to you.

Trust deepens our relationship with God. The more we learn to trust and believe everything He says, the closer we become. We learn over time that He is the Master Controller in charge of everything. Our Heavenly Father can keep us through any given situation. Isn't it good to know that our God is a Keeper! He keeps us through the sacrificial blood of His Son 365 days of the year. The blood of Jesus will never lose its power. Know without a doubt that God will *keep you!*

The Apostle Paul says in Philippians 1:6, *"I am convinced and confident of this very thing, that He who has begun a good work in you will [continue to] perfect and complete it until the day of Christ Jesus [the time of His return]."*

We must stay connected to the vine. Jesus said in John 15:1-7, *"I am the true Vine, and My Father is the vinedresser. Every branch in Me that does not bear fruit, He takes away; and every* branch *that continues to bear fruit, He [repeatedly] prunes, so that it will bear more fruit [even richer and finer fruit]. You are already clean because of the word which I have given you [the teachings which I have discussed with you]. Remain in Me, and I [will remain] in you. Just as no branch can bear fruit by itself without remaining in the vine, neither can you [bear fruit, producing evidence of your faith] unless you remain in Me. I am the Vine; you are the branches. The one who remains in Me and I in him bears much fruit, for [otherwise] apart from Me [that is, cut off from vital union with Me] you can do nothing. If anyone does not remain in Me, he is thrown out like a [broken off] branch, and* withers and *dies; and they gather such branches and throw them into the fire, and they are burned. If you remain in Me and My words remain in you [that is, if we are vitally united and My message lives in your heart], ask whatever you wish and it will be done for you."*

We must stay connected to Jesus Christ who is the True Vine for miracles to manifest in our lives and to receive forgiveness when we fall short. When we know the voice of God, our lives will be renewed with a fresh beginning. The Lord becomes our Advocate with the Father as well as the peace of our souls. We need not be overcome with the cares of this world and fall to pieces as if we have no God; because the Lord is our refuge and strength. Through our relationship with Christ, we have access to the kingdom of God.

"For the kingdom of God is not meat and drink, but righteousness, and peace, and joy in the Holy Ghost." (Romans 14:17).

When our relationship matures in the things of the Lord, the love that He has for us will be communicated to others. Even if people do not know Him, they can sense His presence through us sharing the greatest love of all.

"Greater love hath no man than this, that a man lay down his life for his friends. Ye are my friends, if ye do whatsoever I command you. Henceforth I call you not servants; for the servant knoweth not what his lord doeth: but I have called you friends; for all things that I have heard of my Father

I have made known unto you. Ye have not chosen me, but I have chosen you, and ordained you, that ye should go and bring forth fruit, and that your fruit should remain: that whatsoever ye shall ask of the Father in my name, he may give it you." (John 15:13-16).

These are commandments that the Lord gave to us to help add to the kingdom of God. As we are obedient to the call, He will continue to make a way where there appears to be no way. Even when it seems that all odds are against us, we have an Advocate with the Father.

Just keep in mind that God did not call us to be comfortable always. Oftentimes, He will orchestrate a situation in our lives to keep us working, thinking, praying, fasting, and worshipping Him. Why, do you ask? So that we will remember to depend on Him in every situation and for everything that we need; especially when it feels like we are sheep amid ravenous wolves. During those times, we must speak the Word only and continue to trust God to intervene on our behalf. We do not have to fight on our own because the battle belongs to the Lord. However, our responsibility is to be so in tune with the voice of God that we know what to do because we pray and continue to seek His face. If you are not sure quite what to pray the Holy Spirit will remind you of the right words to pray while you are yet praying. If you have been blessed with your Heavenly language (a language that God gives you to speak directly to Him) the enemy will not understand what you are praying. Praying in tongues makes you stronger in your inner man and builds your faith. Use your language often in your private time with the Lord because it is your secret weapon against the attacks of the enemy.

    I was praying early one morning before the break of a new day and the Lord laid it on my heart to pray most of the time in tongues. Thank God that the Lord knows what we have need of even if we do not. He watches over us at every moment no matter what is happening or how alone we may feel. There is a time to pray in our Heavenly language.

Praying loudly in tongues during a church service is unprofitable unless God gives the understanding through another yielded vessel. Our prayer language is a personal gift from God to build us up in our most Holy faith. Being blessed to pray in tongues gives you the strength to keep pressing forward; knowing that God is indeed with you and aware of your current circumstance.

Just bear in mind that when things are going crazy nothing can separate you from the love of God. Even if you feel alone and that no one understands what you are going through, the Lord will be with you. When the truth of God abiding in you saturates your mind and heart, you will be able to go through times of testing with the peace of God.

His voice and very presence will keep you during traumatic times and usher you into an even more intimate relationship with Him. I speak from experience. Trust, as I said earlier, is an action word that requires knowing Jesus beyond the surface.

"Trust in the Lord with all thine heart; and lean not unto thine own understanding. In all thy ways acknowledge him, and he shall direct thy paths." (Proverbs 3:5-6).

Trusting in Him involves being confident in God and leaning on Him for support. Rejoice in the Lord who supports you so strongly and loves you so tenderly.

'For I am convinced [and continue to be convinced—beyond any doubt] that neither death, nor life, nor angels, nor principalities, nor things present and *threatening, nor things to come, nor powers, nor height, nor depth, nor any other created thing, will be able to separate us from the [unlimited] love of God, which is in Christ Jesus our Lord. I am convinced that neither death nor life neither angels nor demons neither the present nor the future, nor any powers neither height nor depths, nor anything else in all creation will be able to separate us from the love of God that is in Christ Jesus our Lord."* (Romans 8-38-39).

The enemy will come in all shapes and sizes, but the Lord is our defense.

"But the Lord has become my high tower and *defense, And my God the rock of my refuge."* (Psalms 94:22).

Do you feel abandoned by God? Pause for a moment and be reminded of the promises in the Scriptures that nothing can separate us from the love of God. Re-read the Bible verses above and be encouraged that Jesus is your rock of refuge.

"Have I not commanded you? Be strong and courageous! Do not be terrified or dismayed (intimidated), for the Lord your God is with you wherever you go." (Joshua 1:9).

Choose faith over fear! Did you know anxiety works just like faith but in favor of the enemy? Faith opens the door for God to work in our lives, but fear opens the door for our adversary to work in our lives. The Bible says that fear has torment and has no mercy. If you act out of fear instead of living by faith, depression, miserableness, and loneliness will manifest in your life.

So many people today are missing out on Gods joy, peace, and victory because they keep giving in to fear. They feed fear by what they watch on TV or at the movies, worrying about and dwelling on bad things. The cares of this world can become so intense that our flesh can get the best of us, causing us to be troubled in our spirit wavering in our faith. During those times, *One Thing is Needful*, and that is the Word of God!

"Faith cometh by hearing and hearing by the word of God." (Romans 20:17).

The more you fill your heart and mind with Gods Word, the stronger you will become to stand against the powers of darkness. Remember the power that is in you is greater than the power of fear. When thoughts come that says that you are not able, choose faith by saying, *"I can do all things [which He has called me to do] through Him who strengthens and empowers me [to fulfill His purpose—I am self-sufficient in Christ's sufficiency; I am ready for anything and equal to anything through Him who infuses me with inner strength and confident peace.]* (Philippians 4:13).

Choose faith today so you can overcome fear and live in the freedom and victory that God has for you through knowing His voice!

Prayer:

Lord Jesus, I receive what Your Word is saying to me which is life, health, and strength. I choose to close the door of fear by guarding what I say, what I listen to and what I dwell on. Continue to fill me Lord with your love and faith as I meditate on Your Word. I understand now that *One Thing is Needful,* and that is the Word of God!

Acknowledgments

I give all the glory, honor and praise to my Heavenly Father for being so kind and merciful unto me. I thank my mother and father for raising and loving me to the best of their ability. I thank my mother for instilling in my heart to have a relationship with Jesus. My mother and father are deceased and so are all four of my brothers. So, now, it's just my older sister and me. I am the youngest. I thank God for my family and what He allowed me to see, learn and understand. I thank God for moving on my behalf and bringing me through the worst of times to the best of times.

INDEX

911, 23
abiding, 114
abundant life, 65, 82, 107
accidents, 59
advice, 29
afflictions, 86
alcohol, 8
alone, iii, 8, 11, 25, 29, 44, 71, 113
anointing, 18
anxiety, 116
battles, 107
Bible, 2, 17, 29, 32, 34, 35, 43, 44, 45, 62, 76, 78, 81, 90, 95, 98, 116, 117
Bishop, T. D. Jakes, 19
bless, 31, 40, 69, 75
blessed, 6, 13, 15, 16, 20, 68, 69, 78, 112, 113
bound, 9, 10, 75
brand-new, 20
broken-hearted, 69
brother, 12, 22, 23
brothers, 7, 103, 121

caretaker, 21
Church, 13, 14, 16, 17, 20, 29
change, 11, 13, 20, 21, 32, 47, 55, 59, 102, 106
chaos, 51, 53
Christ, 10, 16, 28, 32, 40, 41, 42, 48, 62, 74, 75, 78, 79, 86, 88, 89, 90, 91, 92, 96, 100, 101, 102, 103, 104, 108, 109, 115, 118
Christians, 38
cigarettes, 6, 13, 14
clubs, 6, 10
communicate, 90
compass, 35
confession, 39, 67, 89
connection, 10
conscious, 71
consistent, 60, 96
covenant, 17
crisis, 91
crowd, 6, 71
Dallas, 17, 19

INDEX

darkness, 7, 8, 9, 15, 58, 62, 74, 82, 86, 118
death, 38, 57, 59, 64, 68, 79, 82, 103, 115
deliver, 8, 60, 74, 75
deliverance, 25, 69
delivered, 13, 15, 53, 75
destruction, 57
devastation, 31, 34
diligence, 91
direction, 24, 29
disciples, 53
discipline, 102
distractions, 34, 38
divine plan, 89
Dodge Shadow, 59
doubt, 49, 107, 115
drugs, 8
Earth, 9, 38, 45, 70
effective, 63
eighteen-wheeler, 59
Electronics, 6, 34
empty, 13
encourage, iii, 15, 31, 49, 63, 105
encouraging, 11
enemy, 9, 34, 38, 42, 43, 50, 51, 56, 59, 62, 68, 92, 99, 106, 112, 115, 116
eternal life, 34
eternity, 38, 58, 76

evidence, 65, 67, 87, 89, 108
faith, iii, 23, 27, 32, 38, 39, 57, 62, 67, 76, 79, 85, 87, 88, 89, 90, 91, 96, 108, 112, 113, 116, 117, 118, 119
family, 7, 10, 14, 27, 38, 49, 65, 67, 84, 86, 91, 121
Father's Day, 21
fear, 49, 96, 116, 117, 118, 119
feet, 25, 29, 56
finances, 28, 29
finish line, 86
focus, 38, 42, 91
forgiveness, 50, 64, 65, 109
free, 9, 10, 13, 52, 74, 75
friend, 11, 12, 15, 16, 31, 36, 38, 47, 91
friends, 6, 10, 12, 29, 49, 55, 110
glory, 9, 10, 14, 16, 27, 28, 30, 48, 59, 90, 121
God, iii, 5, 7, 8, 9, 10, 12, 13, 14, 15, 16, 17, 18, 19, 22, 24, 26, 27, 28, 29, 30, 31, 32, 33,

34, 35, 37, 38, 39, 40, 41, 42, 43, 44, 45, 48, 49, 50, 51, 52, 53, 56, 57, 58, 59, 60, 62, 63, 65, 66, 67, 68, 69, 70, 71, 74, 75, 76, 77, 78, 79, 81, 82, 83, 84, 86, 87, 88, 89, 91, 93, 95, 96, 97, 98, 99, 100, 101, 102, 103, 105, 106, 107, 109, 110, 111, 113, 114, 115, 116, 117, 118, 119, 121
Gospel, 90
grace, 40, 52, 56, 60, 65, 74, 78, 84, 96, 102
Growing, 6
guidance, 35
heal, 29
health, 28, 65, 69, 118
heart attack, 23
Heavenly Father, 56, 107, 121
help, 8, 15, 18, 22, 25, 29, 35, 38, 39, 49, 52, 57, 60, 61, 81, 90, 100, 111
honor, 18, 83, 101, 121
instructions, 34, 62
intercede, 30
irritated, 25
jealous, 25
Jesus, iii, 9, 10, 11, 16, 17, 22, 24, 25, 26, 28, 29, 31, 36, 37, 39, 40, 41, 42, 47, 48, 50, 51, 52, 53, 55, 56, 57, 58, 59, 61, 62, 63, 65, 66, 67, 74, 78, 79, 82, 84, 85, 86, 88, 90, 92, 96, 97, 103, 106, 107, 108, 109, 114, 115, 116, 118, 121
jobs, 6
judgment, 43, 44
Lake of Fire, 33, 58
Lewisville, 16, 17
light, 15, 41, 62, 65, 74, 82, 86
lilies, 27, 28, 51
Lambs Book of Life, 57
Lord, 2, 6, 9, 10, 12, 13, 14, 15, 17, 19, 21, 23, 25, 26, 28, 29, 31, 36, 37, 39, 40, 41, 43, 47, 48, 50, 55, 56, 57, 61, 63, 65, 66, 67, 68, 69, 74, 75, 76, 77, 78, 80, 84, 85, 86, 90, 92, 98, 99, 101, 105, 109, 110, 111, 112, 113, 114, 115, 116, 118

Lord Jesus Christ, 26, 29, 31, 40, 63, 67, 86
maturity, 41, 92
meditate, iii, 31, 119
MegaCare Outreach Ministry, 20
mercy, 8, 58, 64, 84, 117
mind, 10, 22, 28, 30, 32, 42, 50, 51, 58, 73, 76, 84, 99, 102, 111, 113, 118
miracle, 48, 67
mistakes, 30, 64, 96
Minister, 15, 16, 20, 77
mother, 5, 7, 9, 14, 21, 22, 23, 121
Mother's Day, 23
movies, 20, 34, 117
never forget, 11, 12, 47
offense, 50
One Thing is, 2, 34, 63, 66, 78, 93, 117, 119
One Thing is Needful, 2, 34, 63, 66, 78, 93, 117, 119
opened doors, 30
opportunities, 78, 106
opposition, 91
Persevering, 86

peace, 31, 41, 53, 59, 63, 83, 86, 107, 109, 110, 114, 117, 118
planted, 83, 101
positive, 19, 32
power and authority, 25
praise, 36, 42, 121
pray, 12, 13, 15, 30, 31, 40, 61, 64, 65, 67, 112, 113
prayed, 14, 24, 29, 82
prayer, 13, 15, 26, 28, 30, 39, 41, 49, 56, 57, 67, 97, 105, 113
prayer line, 15, 30, 49
praying, 7, 8, 15, 30, 100, 102, 111, 113
preach, 17, 31, 39, 56, 65
preacher, 11, 12, 16, 47
precious vessels, 30
principalities, 8, 115
priorities, 35
priority, 65, 86
prison, 20
prisoner, 74
problem, 29
process, 43, 84
promises, 67, 68, 97, 105, 116
protected, 9, 21

provides, 2, 20, 34, 82, 98
purpose, 16, 17, 43, 61, 81, 89, 118
radio, 11, 12, 14, 15, 47
reading, iii, 22, 31, 43, 79, 102
refuge, 109, 116
relationship, iii, 10, 17, 26, 67, 78, 89, 100, 107, 110, 114, 121
remember, 5, 7, 9, 21, 49, 50, 57, 59, 65, 70, 79, 87, 91, 111
repent, 56, 65
repentance., 39, 77
reputation, 26
revelation, 26, 87, 88
revival, 12, 13, 17
Revival Center, 16
roadmap, 44, 70, 78, 95, 98, 104
run, 10
running, 6, 21, 86
salvation, 39, 40, 62, 78
sanctuary, 20
saved, iii, 15, 39, 67, 76, 78, 79, 82, 92
Savior, 24, 31, 40, 56, 74
scriptures, 28, 105
servant, 24, 37, 110

seven demons, 24
shift, 59, 68
sin, 10, 52, 73, 75, 83, 84
sovereignty, 51
Sowing, 52
Spirit, 8, 16, 20, 21, 49, 55, 56, 57, 58, 63, 71, 73, 74, 78, 82, 84, 87, 88, 92, 97, 100, 102, 103, 112
spiritual warfare, 43
steadfast, 57
strength, 22, 31, 48, 50, 65, 87, 99, 107, 110, 113, 118
strengthen, iii, 28, 76, 91
study, 17, 61, 70, 96
studying, 24, 90
TBN, 40
testimony, 21, 30, 59, 90, 92
thankful, 14, 16, 40, 48, 58, 65, 74, 84
The…Born-Again Hour, 14
The Potter's House, 19
tithes and offerings, 98
tongues, 112, 113
transformation, 102
treasure, 45

INDEX

Trust, 28, 106, 107, 114
unbelief, 49
unforgiveness, 100
victim, 82
victorious, 55, 68
weapon, 68, 112
wind, 13
Winning, 86

witness, 63, 92
Word of God, iii, 9, 10, 22, 31, 34, 35, 39, 44, 45, 48, 66, 68, 70, 71, 82, 83, 97, 106
worry, 28, 49
worship, 17, 20

Prayer Line

Jesus is Highly Recommended Prayer Line

Monday Through Friday
9:00 AM (CST)

Call

1.515.739.1038

Enter Code

994501#

If this book has blessed you,
please share it with your family and friends, and
others you would like to bless.

~

Thank you!